50 Midnight Meals: Cooking After Dark

By: Kelly Johnson

Table of Contents

- Late-Night Ramen
- Midnight Mac and Cheese
- Spicy Tofu Stir-Fry
- Garlic Butter Shrimp Tacos
- Crispy Fried Chicken Sliders
- Grilled Cheese and Tomato Soup
- Truffle Popcorn
- Spicy Sriracha Fries
- Midnight Pizzas
- Sweet and Savory Waffles
- Bacon-Wrapped Jalapeño Poppers
- Kimchi Fries
- Miso Soup with a Twist
- Cheese-Stuffed Pretzel Bites
- Instant Pot Beef Stew
- Poutine with Extra Cheese
- Breakfast for Dinner: Omelet Surprise

- Fried Rice and Eggs
- Sweet Potato Nachos
- Spicy Queso Dip and Chips
- Midnight Tacos
- Loaded Potato Skins
- Roasted Brussels Sprouts with Balsamic Glaze
- Garlic Parmesan Wings
- Korean BBQ Sliders
- Avocado Toast with Poached Egg
- Chili Cheese Dogs
- Homemade Nachos
- Sloppy Joes with a Kick
- Veggie Stuffed Mushrooms
- Crispy Eggplant Fries
- Mediterranean Hummus Bowls
- Spicy Pimento Cheese Dip
- Mozzarella Sticks with Marinara
- Taco Salad Supreme
- Eggplant Parmesan Bites

- Creamy Spinach Artichoke Dip
- Sweet and Sour Chicken Bites
- Savory Crepes with Spinach and Cheese
- Grilled Portobello Mushrooms
- Loaded Cauliflower Bites
- Sweet and Spicy Popcorn Chicken
- Spicy Peanut Noodles
- Black Bean Burgers
- Chicken Quesadillas
- Cauliflower Buffalo Bites
- Sweet-and-Salty Trail Mix
- Cinnamon Sugar Churros
- Coconut Curry Noodles
- Midnight Pancakes with Maple Bacon

Late-Night Ramen

Ingredients:

- 1 package instant ramen noodles (or fresh ramen)
- 1 boiled egg
- 1/2 cup cooked chicken or pork (optional)
- 1/4 cup sliced mushrooms
- 1/4 cup spinach or bok choy
- 2 tbsp soy sauce
- 1 tsp sesame oil
- 1 tbsp miso paste (optional)
- 1 tsp chili oil (for a spicy kick)
- 1/2 tsp sesame seeds

Instructions:

1. Cook ramen noodles according to the package instructions.
2. While the noodles are cooking, sauté mushrooms and spinach in sesame oil for 2-3 minutes until tender.
3. Once noodles are cooked, add soy sauce, miso paste (if using), and chili oil to the broth.
4. Add cooked chicken or pork, mushrooms, and spinach to the soup.
5. Top with a boiled egg, sprinkle sesame seeds, and serve hot!

Midnight Mac and Cheese

Ingredients:

- 2 cups elbow macaroni
- 1 cup shredded sharp cheddar cheese
- 1/2 cup milk
- 2 tbsp butter
- 1 tbsp flour
- 1/4 tsp garlic powder
- Salt and pepper to taste
- 1/4 cup breadcrumbs (optional)

Instructions:

1. Cook the macaroni according to the package instructions and drain.
2. In a separate saucepan, melt butter over medium heat. Stir in the flour and cook for 1-2 minutes.
3. Gradually add the milk, stirring constantly to avoid lumps. Bring to a simmer and cook for another 2-3 minutes until thickened.
4. Stir in the shredded cheese, garlic powder, salt, and pepper. Continue stirring until the cheese melts and the sauce is smooth.
5. Combine the sauce with the cooked macaroni and stir to coat. Top with breadcrumbs and bake at 375°F (190°C) for 10 minutes if you want a crispy topping.

Spicy Tofu Stir-Fry

Ingredients:

- 1 block firm tofu, cubed
- 1 tbsp soy sauce
- 1 tbsp sriracha sauce
- 1 tbsp sesame oil
- 1/2 cup bell peppers, sliced
- 1/4 cup onion, sliced
- 1/4 cup carrots, julienned
- 2 cloves garlic, minced
- 1 tbsp honey
- 1 tsp sesame seeds

Instructions:

1. Press the tofu to remove excess moisture and cut it into cubes.
2. Heat sesame oil in a large pan and sauté tofu until golden and crispy on all sides. Remove tofu and set aside.
3. In the same pan, add garlic, onion, bell peppers, and carrots. Stir-fry for 3-4 minutes.
4. Stir in soy sauce, sriracha, honey, and tofu. Cook for another 2-3 minutes until everything is coated in the sauce.
5. Sprinkle with sesame seeds and serve hot over rice or noodles.

Garlic Butter Shrimp Tacos

Ingredients:

- 1 lb shrimp, peeled and deveined
- 2 tbsp butter
- 2 cloves garlic, minced
- 1 tsp paprika
- 1/2 tsp chili flakes
- 1 tbsp lime juice
- 8 small tortillas
- 1/2 cup shredded lettuce
- 1/4 cup diced tomatoes
- 1/4 cup chopped cilantro

Instructions:

1. In a pan, melt butter over medium heat. Add garlic, paprika, and chili flakes. Cook for 1 minute.
2. Add shrimp and cook for 3-4 minutes until pink and cooked through. Stir in lime juice.
3. Warm tortillas and top each with shrimp, lettuce, tomatoes, and cilantro.
4. Serve with a squeeze of lime.

Crispy Fried Chicken Sliders

Ingredients:

- 4 chicken tenders (or small chicken breasts)
- 1 cup buttermilk
- 1 cup all-purpose flour
- 1 tsp paprika
- 1 tsp garlic powder
- 1/2 tsp cayenne pepper
- Salt and pepper to taste
- 1 cup vegetable oil (for frying)
- 4 slider buns
- Pickles and mayo (for garnish)

Instructions:

1. Marinate the chicken in buttermilk for at least 30 minutes (or overnight).
2. In a bowl, mix flour, paprika, garlic powder, cayenne, salt, and pepper.
3. Dredge the chicken tenders in the flour mixture.
4. Heat oil in a frying pan over medium-high heat and fry chicken until golden and crispy (about 4-5 minutes per side).
5. Assemble the sliders by placing fried chicken on the buns, topping with pickles and mayo. Serve immediately.

Grilled Cheese and Tomato Soup

Ingredients (for the sandwich):

- 2 slices bread
- 2 tbsp butter
- 2 slices cheddar cheese

Ingredients (for the soup):

- 1 can (14 oz) crushed tomatoes
- 1/2 cup vegetable broth
- 1 tsp olive oil
- 1 clove garlic, minced
- Salt and pepper to taste
- 1 tsp dried basil

Instructions:

1. For the soup, heat olive oil in a pot over medium heat. Add garlic and cook for 1 minute.
2. Stir in crushed tomatoes, vegetable broth, salt, pepper, and basil. Simmer for 10-15 minutes.
3. For the grilled cheese, butter the bread on both sides and place cheese between the slices.
4. Grill the sandwich in a pan over medium heat until golden brown and the cheese is melted (about 3 minutes per side).

5. Serve the grilled cheese alongside the hot tomato soup.

Truffle Popcorn

Ingredients:

- 1/2 cup popcorn kernels
- 2 tbsp truffle oil
- 1 tbsp butter, melted
- 1/4 cup grated parmesan cheese
- Salt to taste

Instructions:

1. Pop the popcorn using your preferred method (stovetop or air popper).
2. In a large bowl, drizzle the melted butter and truffle oil over the popped popcorn.
3. Toss with parmesan and salt, and serve immediately.

Spicy Sriracha Fries

Ingredients:

- 4 large potatoes, cut into fries
- 2 tbsp olive oil
- 1 tbsp sriracha sauce
- 1 tbsp honey
- Salt to taste
- Fresh cilantro for garnish (optional)

Instructions:

1. Preheat oven to 425°F (220°C). Toss fries in olive oil and spread them out on a baking sheet.
2. Bake for 25-30 minutes, flipping halfway, until crispy and golden.
3. In a small bowl, mix sriracha sauce, honey, and salt. Drizzle over the fries and toss to coat.
4. Garnish with cilantro and serve hot.

Midnight Pizzas

Ingredients:

- 1 pizza dough (store-bought or homemade)
- 1/2 cup pizza sauce
- 1 cup shredded mozzarella cheese
- 1/4 cup pepperoni or any toppings of your choice
- Olive oil for drizzling

Instructions:

1. Preheat oven to 450°F (230°C).
2. Roll out the pizza dough and spread pizza sauce over it.
3. Top with mozzarella cheese and your favorite toppings.
4. Bake for 10-12 minutes, or until the crust is golden and the cheese is bubbly.
5. Drizzle with olive oil before serving.

Sweet and Savory Waffles

Ingredients:

- 1 cup all-purpose flour
- 1 tbsp sugar
- 1 tsp baking powder
- 1/4 tsp salt
- 1 egg
- 1/2 cup milk
- 1/4 cup melted butter
- 1/4 tsp cinnamon
- 1/4 cup chopped bacon
- Maple syrup for drizzling

Instructions:

1. Preheat your waffle iron.
2. In a bowl, mix flour, sugar, baking powder, salt, and cinnamon.
3. In another bowl, whisk together the egg, milk, and melted butter.
4. Combine both mixtures and stir until smooth. Fold in chopped bacon.
5. Pour the batter into the waffle iron and cook until golden and crispy.
6. Serve with a drizzle of maple syrup.

Bacon-Wrapped Jalapeño Poppers

Ingredients:

- 12 jalapeños, halved and seeded
- 8 oz cream cheese, softened
- 1 cup shredded cheddar cheese
- 12 slices bacon
- 1/4 tsp garlic powder
- 1/4 tsp paprika

Instructions:

1. Preheat the oven to 400°F (200°C).
2. In a bowl, mix cream cheese, cheddar cheese, garlic powder, and paprika.
3. Stuff each jalapeño half with the cheese mixture.
4. Wrap each stuffed jalapeño with a slice of bacon and secure with toothpicks.
5. Arrange on a baking sheet and bake for 20-25 minutes until the bacon is crispy.
6. Serve hot and enjoy!

Kimchi Fries

Ingredients:

- 2 cups frozen French fries (or homemade)
- 1/2 cup kimchi, chopped
- 1/4 cup green onions, chopped
- 1 tbsp sesame oil
- 1/4 cup mayonnaise
- 1 tbsp sriracha sauce
- 1 tbsp sesame seeds

Instructions:

1. Cook fries according to package instructions (bake or fry).
2. While fries are cooking, mix mayonnaise, sriracha sauce, and sesame oil in a bowl.
3. Once fries are crispy, top with chopped kimchi, green onions, and drizzle with spicy mayo.
4. Sprinkle with sesame seeds and serve immediately.

Miso Soup with a Twist

Ingredients:

- 4 cups water
- 2 tbsp miso paste (red or white)
- 1/4 cup dried seaweed
- 1/4 cup tofu, cubed
- 1/4 cup green onions, chopped
- 1 tbsp soy sauce
- 1 tsp sesame oil

Instructions:

1. In a pot, bring water to a boil. Stir in miso paste until dissolved.
2. Add tofu, seaweed, soy sauce, and sesame oil. Simmer for 5-7 minutes.
3. Garnish with chopped green onions and serve hot.

Cheese-Stuffed Pretzel Bites

Ingredients:

- 1 package pizza dough (or homemade dough)
- 4 oz mozzarella cheese, cut into cubes
- 1/4 cup baking soda
- 4 cups water
- 1 tbsp melted butter
- Coarse salt for sprinkling

Instructions:

1. Preheat oven to 375°F (190°C).
2. Roll out the pizza dough and cut it into 12 squares.
3. Place a cube of mozzarella in the center of each square and pinch the edges to seal.
4. Bring water to a boil in a pot and add baking soda. Drop the stuffed dough balls into the water for 30 seconds, then remove.
5. Arrange the pretzel bites on a baking sheet and brush with melted butter. Sprinkle with coarse salt.
6. Bake for 15-20 minutes, until golden brown. Serve warm with marinara sauce.

Instant Pot Beef Stew

Ingredients:

- 1 lb beef stew meat, cubed
- 4 cups beef broth
- 3 carrots, sliced
- 2 potatoes, cubed
- 1 onion, chopped
- 3 cloves garlic, minced
- 1 tsp thyme
- 1 tsp rosemary
- 1 tbsp olive oil
- Salt and pepper to taste

Instructions:

1. Set Instant Pot to "Sauté" mode and heat olive oil. Brown the beef stew meat for 5-6 minutes.
2. Add garlic and onion and sauté for another 2 minutes.
3. Add carrots, potatoes, beef broth, thyme, rosemary, salt, and pepper.
4. Seal the Instant Pot and cook on "Pressure Cook" for 30 minutes.
5. Release the pressure, stir, and serve hot.

Poutine with Extra Cheese

Ingredients:

- 2 cups French fries, cooked
- 1 cup cheese curds
- 1 cup beef gravy (homemade or store-bought)
- 1/2 tsp black pepper

Instructions:

1. Prepare the fries and arrange them on a plate.
2. Pour hot beef gravy over the fries and top with cheese curds.
3. Sprinkle with black pepper and serve immediately.

Breakfast for Dinner: Omelet Surprise

Ingredients:

- 4 eggs, beaten
- 1/4 cup milk
- 1/4 cup shredded cheese (cheddar or your choice)
- 1/4 cup cooked bacon or sausage, crumbled
- 1/4 cup diced bell peppers
- 1/4 cup onions, chopped
- Salt and pepper to taste

Instructions:

1. In a bowl, whisk together eggs, milk, salt, and pepper.
2. Pour the mixture into a greased pan and cook over medium heat for 2-3 minutes until the edges begin to set.
3. Sprinkle cheese, bacon, bell peppers, and onions on one half of the omelet.
4. Fold the other half over the fillings and cook for an additional 2-3 minutes until fully set. Serve immediately.

Fried Rice and Eggs

Ingredients:

- 2 cups cooked rice (preferably day-old)
- 2 eggs, beaten
- 1/4 cup peas and carrots (frozen or fresh)
- 2 tbsp soy sauce
- 1 tbsp sesame oil
- 2 cloves garlic, minced
- 1/4 cup green onions, chopped

Instructions:

1. Heat sesame oil in a pan over medium heat. Add garlic and sauté for 1 minute.
2. Add peas and carrots and cook for another 2 minutes.
3. Push the veggies to the side and pour the beaten eggs into the pan. Scramble until cooked.
4. Add cooked rice and soy sauce, stirring everything together.
5. Garnish with green onions and serve hot.

Sweet Potato Nachos

Ingredients:

- 2 medium sweet potatoes, sliced thinly
- 1 tbsp olive oil
- 1/2 tsp paprika
- 1/2 cup black beans, rinsed
- 1/4 cup shredded cheddar cheese
- 1/4 cup sour cream
- 1/4 cup salsa
- 1/4 cup sliced jalapeños (optional)

Instructions:

1. Preheat oven to 400°F (200°C). Toss sweet potato slices in olive oil and paprika. Spread them on a baking sheet.
2. Bake for 20-25 minutes, flipping halfway through until crispy.
3. Top with black beans and shredded cheese. Return to the oven for another 5 minutes until the cheese melts.
4. Top with sour cream, salsa, and jalapeños. Serve immediately.

Spicy Queso Dip and Chips

Ingredients:

- 1 cup shredded cheddar cheese
- 1/2 cup cream cheese
- 1/4 cup salsa
- 1 tbsp jalapeños, minced (optional)
- 1/2 tsp chili powder
- Tortilla chips for dipping

Instructions:

1. In a saucepan over medium heat, melt cream cheese and cheddar cheese together, stirring until smooth.
2. Add salsa, minced jalapeños, and chili powder, and continue stirring until the queso is hot and creamy.
3. Serve the spicy queso dip with tortilla chips for dipping.

Midnight Tacos

Ingredients:

- 1 lb ground beef or chicken
- 1 packet taco seasoning (or homemade seasoning)
- 12 small soft or hard taco shells
- 1 cup shredded lettuce
- 1/2 cup diced tomatoes
- 1/2 cup shredded cheddar cheese
- 1/4 cup sour cream
- Salsa (optional)
- Sliced jalapeños (optional)

Instructions:

1. Cook the ground beef or chicken in a pan over medium heat until browned.
2. Add the taco seasoning and follow the instructions on the packet (or use your own seasoning blend).
3. Warm the taco shells according to the package directions.
4. Fill the taco shells with the cooked meat and top with shredded lettuce, diced tomatoes, cheese, sour cream, salsa, and jalapeños.
5. Serve hot and enjoy!

Loaded Potato Skins

Ingredients:

- 4 medium russet potatoes
- 1/2 cup shredded cheddar cheese
- 1/4 cup cooked bacon, crumbled
- 1/4 cup sour cream
- 2 tbsp chopped green onions
- Salt and pepper to taste
- 1 tbsp olive oil

Instructions:

1. Preheat the oven to 400°F (200°C). Rub the potatoes with olive oil and bake for 45 minutes until soft.

2. Let the potatoes cool slightly, then slice them in half and scoop out most of the flesh, leaving about 1/4 inch of potato.

3. Place the potato skins on a baking sheet and bake for an additional 10 minutes until crispy.

4. Stuff the skins with shredded cheese and crumbled bacon, then return to the oven for another 5 minutes until the cheese melts.

5. Top with sour cream, green onions, and season with salt and pepper. Serve immediately.

Roasted Brussels Sprouts with Balsamic Glaze

Ingredients:

- 1 lb Brussels sprouts, halved
- 2 tbsp olive oil
- Salt and pepper to taste
- 2 tbsp balsamic vinegar
- 1 tbsp honey

Instructions:

1. Preheat the oven to 425°F (220°C). Toss the Brussels sprouts with olive oil, salt, and pepper.
2. Spread them on a baking sheet and roast for 20-25 minutes, flipping halfway through, until crispy and golden.
3. In a small saucepan, combine balsamic vinegar and honey. Bring to a simmer over medium heat until thickened (about 3-4 minutes).
4. Drizzle the balsamic glaze over the roasted Brussels sprouts and serve hot.

Garlic Parmesan Wings

Ingredients:

- 1 lb chicken wings
- 2 tbsp olive oil
- 1/2 cup grated parmesan cheese
- 3 cloves garlic, minced
- 1/4 tsp dried oregano
- 1/4 tsp red pepper flakes
- Salt and pepper to taste

Instructions:

1. Preheat the oven to 400°F (200°C). Toss the wings with olive oil, salt, and pepper, and place them on a baking sheet.
2. Bake the wings for 25-30 minutes, flipping halfway, until crispy.
3. While the wings bake, mix the parmesan cheese, garlic, oregano, and red pepper flakes in a bowl.
4. Once the wings are done, toss them in the garlic parmesan mixture. Serve immediately.

Korean BBQ Sliders

Ingredients:

- 1 lb ground beef or pork
- 2 tbsp soy sauce
- 1 tbsp brown sugar
- 2 cloves garlic, minced
- 1 tbsp sesame oil
- 1/4 cup kimchi, chopped
- 6 slider buns
- 1/4 cup mayo
- 1 tbsp sriracha (optional)

Instructions:

1. Mix the ground beef or pork with soy sauce, brown sugar, garlic, and sesame oil. Form into small patties.
2. Cook the patties in a skillet over medium heat for 3-4 minutes per side until cooked through.
3. Toast the slider buns and mix the mayo with sriracha if desired.
4. Assemble the sliders by spreading spicy mayo on the buns, adding a patty, and topping with chopped kimchi.
5. Serve immediately.

Avocado Toast with Poached Egg

Ingredients:

- 2 slices of whole-grain or sourdough bread
- 1 ripe avocado
- 2 eggs
- 1 tsp lemon juice
- Salt and pepper to taste
- Red pepper flakes (optional)

Instructions:

1. Toast the bread to your desired crispness.
2. Mash the avocado with lemon juice, salt, and pepper.
3. Poach the eggs in simmering water for 3-4 minutes until the whites are set but the yolk remains runny.
4. Spread the mashed avocado on the toasted bread and top with the poached egg.
5. Sprinkle with red pepper flakes (optional) and serve immediately.

Chili Cheese Dogs

Ingredients:

- 4 hot dogs
- 4 hot dog buns
- 1 can chili (or homemade chili)
- 1 cup shredded cheddar cheese
- 1/4 cup diced onions (optional)

Instructions:

1. Grill or cook the hot dogs according to your preference.
2. Heat the chili in a pot on the stove.
3. Toast the buns and place the cooked hot dogs inside.
4. Spoon the hot chili over the hot dogs and top with shredded cheese and diced onions.
5. Serve immediately.

Homemade Nachos

Ingredients:

- 1 bag tortilla chips
- 1 cup shredded cheddar cheese
- 1/2 cup black beans, drained and rinsed
- 1/2 cup diced tomatoes
- 1/4 cup sliced jalapeños
- 1/4 cup sour cream
- Salsa (optional)

Instructions:

1. Preheat the oven to 375°F (190°C). Spread the tortilla chips in an even layer on a baking sheet.
2. Sprinkle the chips with shredded cheddar cheese, black beans, tomatoes, and jalapeños.
3. Bake for 10 minutes, or until the cheese is melted and bubbly.
4. Top with sour cream and salsa. Serve hot.

Sloppy Joes with a Kick

Ingredients:

- 1 lb ground beef or turkey
- 1 onion, chopped
- 1/4 cup ketchup
- 1/4 cup barbecue sauce
- 1 tbsp sriracha sauce
- 1 tbsp Worcestershire sauce
- 1 tsp smoked paprika
- 4 hamburger buns
- Pickles (optional)

Instructions:

1. In a skillet, cook the ground meat and onion over medium heat until browned and the onion is soft.
2. Stir in ketchup, barbecue sauce, sriracha, Worcestershire sauce, and paprika. Simmer for 5-7 minutes.
3. Toast the hamburger buns and spoon the sloppy joe mixture onto the buns.
4. Top with pickles (optional) and serve immediately.

Veggie Stuffed Mushrooms

Ingredients:

- 12 large mushroom caps
- 1/2 cup cream cheese, softened
- 1/4 cup spinach, chopped
- 1/4 cup breadcrumbs
- 1/4 cup grated parmesan cheese
- 1/4 tsp garlic powder
- Salt and pepper to taste

Instructions:

1. Preheat the oven to 375°F (190°C).
2. Remove the stems from the mushrooms and set aside.
3. In a bowl, mix cream cheese, spinach, breadcrumbs, parmesan, garlic powder, salt, and pepper.
4. Stuff the mushroom caps with the mixture and arrange them on a baking sheet.
5. Bake for 15-20 minutes, or until golden and bubbly. Serve hot.

Crispy Eggplant Fries

Ingredients:

- 1 large eggplant, cut into fries
- 1/2 cup breadcrumbs
- 1/2 cup grated parmesan cheese
- 1 egg, beaten
- 1/2 tsp garlic powder
- Salt and pepper to taste
- Olive oil for drizzling

Instructions:

1. Preheat the oven to 425°F (220°C). Line a baking sheet with parchment paper.
2. In a bowl, combine breadcrumbs, parmesan, garlic powder, salt, and pepper.
3. Dip the eggplant fries into the beaten egg, then coat them in the breadcrumb mixture.
4. Arrange the fries on the baking sheet and drizzle with olive oil.
5. Bake for 20-25 minutes, flipping halfway, until crispy. Serve with marinara sauce or your favorite dip.

Mediterranean Hummus Bowls

Ingredients:

- 1 cup hummus (store-bought or homemade)
- 1/2 cup diced cucumber
- 1/2 cup cherry tomatoes, halved
- 1/4 cup Kalamata olives, pitted and sliced
- 1/4 cup feta cheese, crumbled
- 1/4 cup red onion, thinly sliced
- 1 tbsp olive oil
- 1 tbsp lemon juice
- 1 tsp dried oregano
- Fresh parsley for garnish
- Pita chips or pita bread for serving

Instructions:

1. Spread the hummus evenly in a shallow bowl or plate.
2. Arrange the cucumber, tomatoes, olives, feta cheese, and red onion on top of the hummus.
3. Drizzle with olive oil and lemon juice, then sprinkle with dried oregano.
4. Garnish with fresh parsley and serve with pita chips or pita bread for dipping.

Spicy Pimento Cheese Dip

Ingredients:

- 8 oz cream cheese, softened
- 1 cup shredded sharp cheddar cheese
- 1/2 cup mayonnaise
- 1/4 cup pimentos, chopped
- 1-2 tbsp pickled jalapeños, chopped (adjust to desired spiciness)
- 1/2 tsp garlic powder
- 1/2 tsp onion powder
- Salt and pepper to taste
- Crushed red pepper flakes (optional)

Instructions:

1. In a medium bowl, mix together the cream cheese, shredded cheddar cheese, and mayonnaise until smooth.
2. Stir in the chopped pimentos, pickled jalapeños, garlic powder, onion powder, salt, and pepper.
3. Taste and adjust seasoning with additional salt, pepper, or red pepper flakes if desired.
4. Serve with crackers, veggie sticks, or toasted bread.

Mozzarella Sticks with Marinara

Ingredients:

- 12 mozzarella cheese sticks
- 1 cup all-purpose flour
- 2 eggs, beaten
- 1 cup breadcrumbs (preferably Italian-style)
- 1/2 tsp garlic powder
- 1/2 tsp dried oregano
- 1/2 tsp salt
- 1/4 tsp black pepper
- Vegetable oil for frying
- 1 cup marinara sauce (for dipping)

Instructions:

1. Freeze the mozzarella sticks for at least 1 hour to prevent them from melting during frying.
2. Set up a breading station: in one bowl, place the flour; in another, the beaten eggs; and in a third, the breadcrumbs mixed with garlic powder, oregano, salt, and pepper.
3. Dip each frozen mozzarella stick into the flour, then the eggs, and then the breadcrumbs, pressing to coat evenly.
4. Heat oil in a deep fryer or large skillet over medium heat.

5. Fry the mozzarella sticks in batches for about 2-3 minutes, or until golden and crispy.

6. Remove and drain on paper towels. Serve hot with marinara sauce for dipping.

Taco Salad Supreme

Ingredients:

- 1 lb ground beef or turkey
- 1 packet taco seasoning (or homemade seasoning)
- 1 head romaine lettuce, chopped
- 1 cup cherry tomatoes, halved
- 1/2 cup shredded cheddar cheese
- 1/4 cup red onion, thinly sliced
- 1/2 cup black beans, drained and rinsed
- 1/2 cup corn kernels (fresh, frozen, or canned)
- 1/2 cup crushed tortilla chips
- 1/4 cup sour cream
- 1/4 cup salsa
- 1 tbsp fresh cilantro, chopped

Instructions:

1. Cook the ground beef or turkey in a skillet over medium heat until browned. Add the taco seasoning and water according to package instructions, and cook until thickened.
2. In a large bowl, combine the chopped lettuce, tomatoes, shredded cheese, red onion, black beans, and corn.
3. Add the cooked meat mixture to the salad and toss gently.

4. Top with crushed tortilla chips, sour cream, salsa, and cilantro.

5. Serve immediately for a delicious and fresh taco salad.

Eggplant Parmesan Bites

Ingredients:

- 1 large eggplant, sliced into 1/2-inch rounds
- 1 cup breadcrumbs
- 1/2 cup grated parmesan cheese
- 1 cup marinara sauce
- 1 cup shredded mozzarella cheese
- 2 eggs, beaten
- Olive oil for frying
- Fresh basil for garnish

Instructions:

1. Preheat the oven to 400°F (200°C). Line a baking sheet with parchment paper.
2. Dip each eggplant slice into the beaten eggs, then coat with breadcrumbs and parmesan cheese.
3. Heat olive oil in a skillet over medium heat and fry the eggplant slices for 2-3 minutes per side until golden.
4. Arrange the fried eggplant on the baking sheet, then top each piece with a spoonful of marinara sauce and shredded mozzarella cheese.
5. Bake for 5-7 minutes, or until the cheese is melted and bubbly.
6. Garnish with fresh basil and serve as bite-sized appetizers.

Creamy Spinach Artichoke Dip

Ingredients:

- 8 oz cream cheese, softened
- 1/2 cup sour cream
- 1/2 cup mayonnaise
- 1 cup frozen spinach, thawed and drained
- 1 can (14 oz) artichoke hearts, drained and chopped
- 1 cup shredded mozzarella cheese
- 1/2 cup grated parmesan cheese
- 1/4 tsp garlic powder
- Salt and pepper to taste

Instructions:

1. Preheat the oven to 375°F (190°C).
2. In a medium bowl, mix together the cream cheese, sour cream, mayonnaise, spinach, artichokes, mozzarella, parmesan, garlic powder, salt, and pepper.
3. Transfer the mixture to a baking dish and bake for 25-30 minutes, or until bubbly and golden on top.
4. Serve warm with tortilla chips, crackers, or vegetable sticks.

Sweet and Sour Chicken Bites

Ingredients:

- 1 lb chicken breast, cut into bite-sized pieces
- 1/2 cup cornstarch
- 1/2 cup all-purpose flour
- 1 egg, beaten
- 1/4 cup vegetable oil (for frying)
- 1/2 cup sweet and sour sauce (store-bought or homemade)

Instructions:

1. In a bowl, mix cornstarch, flour, salt, and pepper. Dip each chicken piece into the beaten egg, then coat with the flour mixture.
2. Heat the vegetable oil in a skillet over medium-high heat and fry the chicken pieces in batches for 3-4 minutes per side, until golden brown and cooked through.
3. Remove the chicken from the skillet and drain on paper towels.
4. Toss the cooked chicken in the sweet and sour sauce and serve immediately.

Savory Crepes with Spinach and Cheese

Ingredients:

- 1 cup all-purpose flour
- 1 1/2 cups milk
- 2 eggs
- 1 tbsp butter, melted
- 1/4 tsp salt
- 1 cup cooked spinach, squeezed dry
- 1/2 cup ricotta cheese
- 1/2 cup shredded mozzarella cheese
- 1/4 cup grated parmesan cheese
- Salt and pepper to taste

Instructions:

1. In a bowl, whisk together the flour, milk, eggs, melted butter, and salt to make the crepe batter.
2. Heat a non-stick skillet over medium heat and lightly grease with butter or oil. Pour 1/4 cup of batter into the pan and swirl to coat the bottom.
3. Cook for 1-2 minutes on each side, then set aside.
4. In a separate bowl, mix the spinach, ricotta, mozzarella, parmesan, salt, and pepper.

5. Spoon the spinach and cheese mixture into the center of each crepe, fold the sides, and serve warm.

Grilled Portobello Mushrooms

Ingredients:

- 4 large portobello mushroom caps
- 2 tbsp olive oil
- 1 tbsp balsamic vinegar
- 1 tsp garlic powder
- 1 tsp dried thyme
- Salt and pepper to taste

Instructions:

1. Preheat the grill or grill pan over medium heat.
2. Brush the mushroom caps with olive oil, balsamic vinegar, garlic powder, thyme, salt, and pepper.
3. Grill the mushrooms for 4-5 minutes on each side, until tender and cooked through.
4. Serve as a side dish or on top of a salad for a satisfying meal.

Loaded Cauliflower Bites

Ingredients:

- 1 medium cauliflower, cut into bite-sized florets
- 1/2 cup flour (or gluten-free flour)
- 1 tsp garlic powder
- 1/2 tsp onion powder
- 1/2 tsp smoked paprika
- Salt and pepper to taste
- 1/2 cup plant-based milk (or regular milk)
- 1/2 cup shredded cheddar cheese (or dairy-free cheese)
- 1/4 cup sour cream (or dairy-free sour cream)
- 2 tbsp chopped green onions
- 2 tbsp cooked bacon crumbles (optional)
- 1 tbsp fresh parsley, chopped

Instructions:

1. Preheat the oven to 400°F (200°C) and line a baking sheet with parchment paper.
2. In a bowl, whisk together the flour, garlic powder, onion powder, smoked paprika, salt, and pepper. Add the plant-based milk and whisk until smooth.
3. Toss the cauliflower florets in the batter, making sure they're evenly coated. Place them on the baking sheet.

4. Bake for 20-25 minutes, or until the cauliflower is golden and crispy.

5. Once baked, remove from the oven and top with shredded cheese, sour cream, green onions, bacon crumbles (if using), and fresh parsley.

6. Serve warm as a snack or appetizer.

Sweet and Spicy Popcorn Chicken

Ingredients:

- 1 lb chicken breast, cut into bite-sized pieces
- 1/2 cup all-purpose flour
- 1/2 tsp paprika
- 1/2 tsp garlic powder
- Salt and pepper to taste
- 1 egg, beaten
- 1 cup panko breadcrumbs
- 1 tbsp vegetable oil (for frying)

For the Sweet and Spicy Sauce:

- 1/4 cup honey
- 2 tbsp sriracha sauce
- 1 tbsp soy sauce
- 1 tbsp rice vinegar
- 1/2 tsp ginger, grated

Instructions:

1. In a bowl, combine the flour, paprika, garlic powder, salt, and pepper. Dredge the chicken pieces in the seasoned flour, then dip them into the beaten egg, followed by the panko breadcrumbs.

2. Heat vegetable oil in a skillet over medium-high heat. Fry the chicken pieces in batches for 3-4 minutes on each side, or until golden and crispy. Remove and drain on paper towels.

3. In a separate small saucepan, combine all the sweet and spicy sauce ingredients. Heat over low heat, stirring until well combined and warmed through.

4. Toss the crispy chicken in the sweet and spicy sauce until well coated.

5. Serve immediately with your favorite dipping sauce or over rice.

Spicy Peanut Noodles

Ingredients:

- 8 oz rice noodles or spaghetti
- 1/4 cup peanut butter
- 2 tbsp soy sauce
- 1 tbsp sriracha sauce (adjust to spice preference)
- 1 tbsp honey or maple syrup
- 1 tbsp sesame oil
- 1 clove garlic, minced
- 1 tsp grated ginger
- 1/4 cup water (or more to thin out the sauce)
- 2 tbsp chopped peanuts (for garnish)
- 1 tbsp chopped green onions (for garnish)
- Lime wedges (for serving)

Instructions:

1. Cook the rice noodles or spaghetti according to package instructions, then drain and set aside.
2. In a large bowl, whisk together the peanut butter, soy sauce, sriracha, honey, sesame oil, garlic, ginger, and water until smooth and creamy.
3. Add the cooked noodles to the bowl and toss to coat them with the peanut sauce.

4. Garnish with chopped peanuts and green onions.

5. Serve with lime wedges for a fresh citrusy zing.

Black Bean Burgers

Ingredients:

- 2 cans (15 oz each) black beans, drained and mashed
- 1/2 cup breadcrumbs
- 1/4 cup grated carrot
- 1/4 cup chopped onion
- 2 cloves garlic, minced
- 1 tsp cumin
- 1 tsp smoked paprika
- 1/2 tsp chili powder
- Salt and pepper to taste
- 1 tbsp olive oil (for cooking)
- Burger buns and toppings (lettuce, tomato, pickles, etc.)

Instructions:

1. In a large bowl, combine the mashed black beans, breadcrumbs, grated carrot, chopped onion, garlic, cumin, smoked paprika, chili powder, salt, and pepper.
2. Mix well and form into patties (about 4-6 patties depending on size).
3. Heat olive oil in a skillet over medium heat. Cook the patties for 4-5 minutes per side, until golden brown and crispy.
4. Serve the black bean burgers on buns with your favorite toppings such as lettuce, tomato, pickles, and sauce.

Chicken Quesadillas

Ingredients:

- 2 cups cooked chicken, shredded
- 1 cup shredded cheese (cheddar, Monterey Jack, or a blend)
- 1/2 cup diced bell pepper
- 1/4 cup diced onion
- 1/2 tsp cumin
- 1/2 tsp chili powder
- Salt and pepper to taste
- 4 flour tortillas
- 1 tbsp olive oil (for cooking)
- Sour cream and salsa for serving

Instructions:

1. In a bowl, combine the shredded chicken, cheese, bell pepper, onion, cumin, chili powder, salt, and pepper.
2. Heat a skillet over medium heat and lightly coat with olive oil.
3. Place one tortilla in the skillet, then spread the chicken mixture evenly on top. Place another tortilla on top and cook for 2-3 minutes per side, or until golden brown and the cheese is melted.
4. Remove from the skillet and cut into wedges. Serve with sour cream and salsa.

Cauliflower Buffalo Bites

Ingredients:

- 1 medium cauliflower, cut into florets
- 1 cup flour
- 1 tsp garlic powder
- 1 tsp onion powder
- 1/2 tsp paprika
- Salt and pepper to taste
- 3/4 cup buffalo sauce
- 2 tbsp melted butter (optional)

Instructions:

1. Preheat the oven to 400°F (200°C) and line a baking sheet with parchment paper.
2. In a bowl, whisk together the flour, garlic powder, onion powder, paprika, salt, and pepper.
3. Dip each cauliflower floret into the flour mixture, then place on the baking sheet.
4. Bake for 20-25 minutes, flipping halfway through, until the cauliflower is golden and crispy.
5. While the cauliflower bakes, mix the buffalo sauce and melted butter (if using) in a bowl.
6. Once the cauliflower is done, toss it in the buffalo sauce until well coated.
7. Serve hot with ranch or blue cheese dressing for dipping.

Sweet-and-Salty Trail Mix

Ingredients:

- 1 cup mixed nuts (almonds, cashews, walnuts, etc.)
- 1/2 cup dried cranberries (or other dried fruit)
- 1/4 cup mini chocolate chips
- 1/4 cup pretzels, broken into pieces
- 1/4 cup roasted salted pumpkin seeds
- 1/4 cup coconut flakes
- 1/2 tsp sea salt
- 1 tbsp honey (optional)

Instructions:

1. In a large bowl, combine the mixed nuts, dried cranberries, chocolate chips, pretzels, pumpkin seeds, and coconut flakes.
2. Sprinkle with sea salt and toss everything together to combine.
3. If you prefer a bit of extra sweetness, drizzle with honey and mix again.
4. Store in an airtight container and enjoy as a snack!

Cinnamon Sugar Churros

Ingredients:

- 1 cup water
- 1/4 cup unsalted butter
- 1 tbsp sugar
- 1/2 tsp salt
- 1 cup all-purpose flour
- 2 large eggs
- 1/4 cup vegetable oil (for frying)

For Cinnamon Sugar Coating:

- 1/2 cup sugar
- 1 tbsp cinnamon

Instructions:

1. In a medium saucepan, bring water, butter, sugar, and salt to a boil over medium heat.
2. Once boiling, stir in the flour until a dough forms and pulls away from the sides of the pan. Remove from heat.
3. Let the dough cool for a few minutes, then beat in the eggs one at a time until smooth and glossy.
4. Heat oil in a deep skillet or pot over medium heat.

5. While the oil heats up, prepare the cinnamon sugar by combining sugar and cinnamon in a shallow bowl.

6. Transfer the dough into a piping bag fitted with a star tip.

7. Carefully pipe strips of dough into the hot oil, cutting them with scissors to the desired length.

8. Fry until golden brown and crispy, about 2-3 minutes per side. Remove with a slotted spoon and drain on paper towels.

9. While still warm, toss the churros in the cinnamon-sugar mixture.

10. Serve immediately with chocolate sauce or caramel for dipping.

Coconut Curry Noodles

Ingredients:

- 8 oz rice noodles (or any noodles of choice)
- 1 tbsp sesame oil
- 1/2 cup onion, diced
- 1 clove garlic, minced
- 1 tbsp grated ginger
- 1 tbsp red curry paste
- 1 can (14 oz) coconut milk
- 1 tbsp soy sauce
- 1 tbsp brown sugar
- 1/2 tsp turmeric
- Salt to taste
- 1/4 cup fresh cilantro, chopped
- Lime wedges for serving

Instructions:

1. Cook the rice noodles according to the package instructions. Drain and set aside.
2. Heat sesame oil in a large skillet over medium heat. Add the onion and sauté for 3-4 minutes until softened.
3. Add the garlic and ginger, cooking for another 1-2 minutes until fragrant.

4. Stir in the red curry paste, coconut milk, soy sauce, brown sugar, and turmeric. Bring the mixture to a simmer.

5. Let the sauce cook for 5-7 minutes until it thickens slightly. Season with salt to taste.

6. Add the cooked noodles to the skillet, tossing to coat in the curry sauce.

7. Top with chopped cilantro and serve with lime wedges on the side.

Midnight Pancakes with Maple Bacon

Ingredients:

- 1 cup all-purpose flour
- 1 tbsp sugar
- 1 tsp baking powder
- 1/2 tsp salt
- 1 egg
- 3/4 cup milk
- 2 tbsp melted butter
- 1/2 tsp vanilla extract
- 6 slices bacon
- 1/4 cup maple syrup (for drizzling)

Instructions:

1. Preheat the oven to 400°F (200°C). Line a baking sheet with parchment paper and place the bacon slices on it.

2. Bake the bacon for 12-15 minutes, or until crispy. Once done, remove from the oven and set aside to drain on paper towels.

3. In a bowl, combine the flour, sugar, baking powder, and salt.

4. In a separate bowl, whisk together the egg, milk, melted butter, and vanilla extract.

5. Pour the wet ingredients into the dry ingredients and stir until just combined (the batter will be lumpy).

6. Heat a non-stick skillet or griddle over medium heat and lightly grease with butter or cooking spray.

7. Pour 1/4 cup of batter onto the skillet for each pancake. Cook for 2-3 minutes on each side until golden brown.

8. Serve the pancakes with crumbled crispy bacon on top and a generous drizzle of maple syrup.

www.ingramcontent.com/pod-product-compliance
Lightning Source LLC
LaVergne TN
LVHW061949070526
838199LV00060B/4033